DISCOVER YOUR CALLING

"It would be crazy to throw a poem to a drowning person. But when a person is drowning in meaninglessness this book could be exactly what he or she needs. Everyone is trying to figure out what to do with the rest of their lives. Almost everyone struggles with this. Most realize that this is not a once-and-it-is-done-forever event in your life but a lifelong process. Dr. Tan has masterfully provided both theory and practice for this. It is seasoned delightfully with generous personal reflections, quotations, and Scripture. I commend this book to anyone wanting some practical help in making sense of their lives."

R. Paul Stevens
Chairman, Institute for Marketplace Transformation; Author of *The Other Six Days: Vocation, Work and Ministry in Biblical Perspective*; *Work Matters*; and *Taking Your Soul to Work*

"This is a book that takes one of humanity's greatest questions 'What is my purpose?' and provides some framing and activities to help each person discover his or her calling. I love that the focus is on the one doing the calling—God; and that it is biblically rich. I also enjoyed the emphasis on discerning one's vocation in community, a necessary corrective to the oft-quoted: 'Follow your heart'! Soo-Inn is wise, and a natural teacher, and this book will give you hope at any stage of your life, as you seek to know His will for your unique abilities and passion. Thoroughly recommended!"

Kara Martin
Lecturer, speaker, and author of *Workship: How to Use Your Work to Worship God*, and *Workship 2: How to Flourish at Work*

"As a pastor, I've been asked how I discovered my calling. I would reply, 'If I tell you how I found my calling to the pastoral ministry, will you share with me how you found your calling to what you are doing now?' Could one be called to be a sales agent, a civil servant, or a homemaker? We attach a glamorous mystique to those in the Christian ministry, but is that biblical?

"Tan Soo-Inn helps us understand that calling by God to our vocation in life is for everyone. Though he spells it out in memorisable steps, the path of discovery is not as easy as ABC. Still, the author, drawing upon his personal experience, and the writings and examples of fellow pilgrims, points us in the direction of finding and fulfilling our God-given mission. A must-read book for all who want to finish well."

Rev. Dr. David W. F. Wong
Leadership Mentor, Finishing Well Ministries

"With enthusiasm and Scripture-saturated wisdom, *Discover Your Calling* is a true encouragement to everyone who hopes to live fully, glorify God, and serve as a vehicle of God's grace in the world. Life today moves so quickly, with kaleidoscopic variety and mediated connectivity, that we are all challenged to slow down, listen to God, and discover our gifts, burdens, and stories. Soo-Inn Tan's wise and practical suggestions for doing so are blessings for disciples of all ages, in all times."

Susan S. Phillips
Sociologist, professor of Christian spirituality, and executive director of New College Berkeley; Author of *The Cultivated Life: From Ceaseless Striving to Receiving Joy*

"Truly a teacher at heart, Soo-Inn clarifies the oft-misunderstood issue of calling in an extremely personal and practical way. For sure, there are many aspects that determine and affect our callings and kingdom assignments. Yet, Soo-Inn masterfully weaves these into an easy-to-understand volume. *Discover Your Calling* is a delightful companion for anyone serious about living purposefully for the Lord."

Henson Lim
Founder, Archippus Awakening

"A book's success is not measured merely by the number of copies it manages to sell. More importantly it is measured by how well the author is able to fulfil the stated purpose for writing the book. Going by this criteria, I consider this book a big success. My friend Dr. Soo-Inn Tan's purpose for this book is 'to provide biblical and practical help for those who want to discover what God may be calling them to do with their lives.' He has ably done that in a relatively short number of chapters.

"For any Christian who seeks to know his or her specific calling in life, this book will definitely be a great help and clear guide. It is biblical, personal, practical, and motivational. It will surely add light to your understanding, fire to your soul, and passion to your heart regarding your specific calling in life."

Pastor Kee-Hing Lam
Associate Pastor, Skyline SIB Church, Kota Kinabalu;
Pastor to Malaysian indigenous leaders

"Many have written about vocational discernment. Some focus on biblical principles. Others focus on practical guidance. However, few provide both in a balanced way. This book is that rare gem that blends both! Dr. Tan Soo-Inn exquisitely weaves together biblical insight with clear guidance as to what steps are needed to discern one's calling. You will also be refreshed by the stories of real people, including the author's, in their journeys of vocational discovery. I recommend this book wholeheartedly."

Lisman Komaladi
General Secretary, Fellowship of Evangelical Students, Singapore

"No one wants to live life without purpose or meaning. Or live life in parts: finding joy in a corner of life, but having the rest walled off in drudgery. But how do you find this illusive meaning? Soo-Inn Tan offers remarkable insight into this journey for discovery, drawing on his own story. He doesn't take us to simple, pat answers. Rather, he prepares the reader for the continuing challenge and joy of a lifelong walk with Jesus Christ across all aspects of vocation. I highly recommend this for those at any stage of the journey."

Albert M. Erisman
Retired Boeing executive; Author of *The ServiceMaster Story: Navigating Tension between People and Profit*, and *The Accidental Executive: Lessons on Business, Faith, and Calling from the Life of Joseph*

"Soo-Inn Tan is a man of deep character who has journeyed closely with God through the mountaintops and valleys of life. A gifted Bible teacher, he's a wise, sensible practitioner—a trustworthy guide for discovering one's vocation no matter your stage of life.

"This book provides biblical and down-to-earth support for all women and men who seek to better understand how God is shaping their lives. It demystifies the discernment process by reinforcing three vital vocational habits: paying attention to abilities, burdens of the heart, and critical incidents of one's life—what Soo-Inn refers to as the A-B-Cs for deciphering calling. Soo-Inn's writing moves quickly, but do not be fooled; this is no superficial treatment. As you work through this important book, you will find yourself changed."

John R. Terrill
Executive Director, Upper House, a Christian study center on the University of Wisconsin—Madison campus, USA

"What is my life purpose? What is my calling?"

"I often hear these burning questions when I come alongside others. Soo-Inn Tan—a dear fellow whole-life mentor in the Lausanne Movement—gives us helpful tools in this book. Rooted in the Scriptures, practical, it draws honest lessons from his own life. As an A-B-C book it guides us to God's calling through our Abilities, Burdens, and Critical life incidents. I wish I had this book earlier, as it has deepened my hunger for Him who has called us into fellowship with His Son, Jesus Christ our Lord."

Ole-Magnus Olafsrud
Chair, Younger Leaders Generation mentoring team, The Lausanne Movement

"This book offers wise, biblical, and practical insights to help Christians discover their sense of life purpose. Rooted in God's calling to follow Jesus and to serve Him with our unique gifts, Soo-Inn Tan provides a spiritually and relationally grounded approach. It deserves thoughtful reflection by young adults, retirees, and everyone in between."

Jeffrey P. Greenman
President, Regent College

"I'm over fifty, and this book was written just for me! I want to be focused and effective at living out my calling. I'm grateful for Pastor Soo-Inn's biblical, practical teaching.

Dan Elliott
Editorial Director, Tyndale House Publishers

"All of us have a yearning to understand where we belong in this world. As Christians most of us understand or believe that God has a purpose for each of us and has gifted each of us differently—both so clear in Scripture. But discovering our unique giftedness and discovering where God calls us to use those gifts eludes so many. Soo-Inn Tan provides here a simple and effective 'A-B-C' framework to help each of us seek clarity in our calling. This has been the investment of a lifetime for stewardship of my own life—and I am thankful for Soo-Inn's own gift of clarity."

Don Foster
CEO, Orphanon Biologics

"For a generation contending with change and confusion, both inside and outside the church, gaining a clearer sense of identity and purpose from God's perspective is essential. This book introduces us to a process for clarifying very specifically what God is inviting each of us to be and to do. Soo-Inn Tan weaves together a rich combination of his own personal experience, biblical wisdom, and insights gained from many of his favourite authors. Numerous writers (including myself) have attempted to do something similar, but very few have succeeded as well as Soo-Inn Tan in so few pages. It is the condensed wisdom and popular presentation that make this book so valuable. Easy to read, but also thoughtful and practical."

Alistair Mackenzie
Author of *Soul Purpose:
Making a Difference in Life and Work*

BOOKS BY THE AUTHOR

Walking With The Risen Christ
3-2-1: Following Jesus in Threes
Friends in a Broken World
Leadership: A Primer
Spiritual Friendship: A Primer
Thinking on the Run
Travel Mercies
Making Sense

DISCOVER YOUR CALLING

THE ABC OF VOCATIONAL DISCERNMENT

Soo-Inn Tan

GRACEWORKS

Discover Your Calling: The ABC of Vocational Discernment

Copyright © 2020 by Soo-Inn Tan

All rights reserved. No part of this publication may be reproduced, stored in a retrieval system, or transmitted, in any form or by any means, electronic, mechanical, photocopying, recording or otherwise, without the prior written permission of the author, except in the case of brief quotations embodied in critical articles and reviews.

Published by Graceworks Private Limited
22 Sin Ming Lane
#04-76 Midview City
Singapore 573969
Tel: 67523403
Email: enquiries@graceworks.com.sg
Website: www.graceworks.com.sg

All Scripture quotations, unless otherwise noted, are taken from The Holy Bible, New International Version®. NIV®. Copyright © 1973, 1978, 1984, 2011 by International Bible Society. Used by permission of Zondervan. All rights reserved.

Typeface: College Stencil, Futura PT, Source Sans Variable

ISBN: 978-981-14-3664-2

2 3 4 5 6 7 8 9 10 • 28 27 26 25 24 23 22 21

CONTENTS

Foreword . . . . *xv*
Acknowledgements . . . . *xxi*
Introduction . . . . *xxiii*

1 What Is Calling? 1
2 How to Discover My Calling? 12
3 What Is My Primary Ability? 24
4 What Is My Primary Burden? 36
5 What Are My Critical Life Incidents? 48
6 The Practice of Vocation 64

Putting It All Together 78
Conclusion 92
Endnotes 98

FOREWORD

Who am I?
Why am I?
What am I to do with my life?

These are the questions for everyone everywhere, whether we ask them consciously or not, whatever our circumstances may be.

Finding people who will give honest answers to these honest questions is harder than most of us imagine—and this is only complicated by the reality that all of us are wounded people living in a wounded world. And sometimes, very sadly, the church does not help as it could and should, and it ends up wounding us too.

For most of 2,000 years the meaning of calling has been controversial, which is almost tragic. As central as it is meant to be in the common life of ordinary people, because of the dualism which has long afflicted the church—in a thousand different ways rupturing the whole of Christian discipleship, fracturing the coherence that we all long for—we are disposed to making some parts of life more important than others. Even worse, we are disposed to believing that God is like us, i.e. that he has called some things "clean" and some things "not clean", some things holy and some things not holy, that some things we do with our lives honors him, and that some things are "less-than", falling short of God's intention for his most serious followers. In some traditions of the church, it is only those who have "religious" work to do who have "vocations"; the rest must simply choose their work. And from my observation, the church all over the world stumbles over this. Catholic, Orthodox, and Protestant, in our very different ways we cannot get this right.

Rather than having a theological vision that sees all of life mattering to God who is the Creator and Redeemer of all of life—in Abraham Kuyper's great words, "every square inch of the whole of reality belongs to Jesus who alone is Lord"—more often than not we have compartmentalized life and faith, assuming and insisting that one is more "secular" and one is more "sacred". Simply said, the biblical vision is this: be holy in all that you are, in all that you do.

I remember a conversation in a summer school class at Regent College where we focused on "vocation" for the week. Doing my best to make the conversation honestly global, drawing on readings and stories that represented the whole world, we made our way through the days, listening to each other, learning from the best people I know. On the last morning, a woman from the other side of the world came up to me in the mid-morning break. It was our first conversation, and I was glad to know more. She told me that she had been plagued by a conundrum for years, and thought that I had answered her question. Of course I wondered what it was! "I have never been able to figure out the relationship between my 'Christian life' and my 'life'." I looked at her, wondering what she had learned. "They're the same, aren't they?" She smiled, and I smiled with her, glad that she had found the coherence she longed for—because of course they are the same.

In this new book by Soo-Inn Tan we are invited to think through why these questions matter for every son of Adam and daughter of Eve. *Who am I? Why am I? What am I to do with my life?* Widely read, the author draws us into his own pilgrimage in"discovering your calling", gracing us with the thoughtful voices that have spoken to him through the years, giving clarity and confidence in making sense of his own vocation. He has lived his own life well, with a holy self-consciousness thinking through his own answers, reading the best books, and learning from the most trusted teachers.

The longer I read, the more sure I was of listening into the story of a calling incarnate, a vocation made flesh in the life of the author—from his own discernment through the years about the work of his life, into the years of his wide reading on the nature of calling. Even to read what he has read would be its own wonderful education!

Why does this matter—whether we are in Vancouver, in Singapore, or in Washington DC? Several years ago I spent a weekend with a group of men at a weekend retreat, one focused on the meaning of vocation. From Friday night through Sunday morning, we labored together, reading the biblical text, doing theological reflection, analyzing the culture and its messages about the work of our lives, and listening to the stories of faithful, thoughtful, visionary folk who see their vocations as integral, not incidental, to the *missio Dei*. When I had finished my last presentation, a group of guys walked up to me and asked if I would meet one of their friends, someone they had invited to the weekend. "Of course," and so we talked for a while. He was British, had lived in New

York City through his adulthood, and had spent the years of his working life in "the space where business and technology meet". Then he said, "I have been serious about my faith since I was in university, wanting what I believe to be worked out in what I do. But I have always felt that the church thought my choice to be in business was 'second-rate', a bit less serious than if I had done something more 'Christian' with my life. I want you to know that a wound in my heart has been healed this weekend."

Yes, sometimes, very sadly, the church ends up wounding us too. We need to be better, we need to do better. And that is why my friend Soo-Inn Tan has written his book, and it is why he has lived his life. I hope many people in many places find their way into learning from this gifted teacher.

Steven Garber
Professor of Marketplace Theology, Regent College;
Author of *The Seamless Life: A Tapestry of Love and Learning, Worship and Work*

ACKNOWLEDGEMENTS

Vocation is pursued in community. I thank God for Bernice who not only reminds me of who I am and what I am called to do, but who sacrificially cares for me as we seek to follow Christ as husband and wife.

I want to thank Don Foster, whose generous sponsorship helped give birth to this book. I am grateful to him and to all our other friends in Seattle for their support and encouragement through the years.

Finally, I want to thank all those who have allowed me to walk with them through the years. Your vocational faithfulness has made it all worthwhile.

INTRODUCTION

William Damon in his book *The Path to Purpose* writes about the importance of helping young people discover their life purpose:

> Purpose endows a person with joy in good times and resilience in hard times, and this holds true all throughout life. Adolescence and emerging adulthood are particularly affected, however, by the presence of purpose, and purposeful youth ... not only avoid the risks of self-destructive behaviour but also show a markedly positive attitude that triggers an eagerness to learn about the world.[1]

In other words, if a young adult understands that his or her life has purpose and has some idea what that purpose may be, it motivates him or her to work at the other aspects of his or her life. It makes sense therefore that we should help young adults begin the journey of discovering what the Lord may be calling them to do.

However, it is not just the young who need to be helped to discover their callings. Pastor Kee-Hing

Lam is committed to helping those 50 and above discover or rediscover their life purpose. He writes:

> I am absolutely convinced that your second half can become the most productive, meaningful and fruitful phase of your life .... However it will not happen automatically! It will only happen when you have discovered your Life Purpose and intentionally use your gifts, talents and resources for helping and blessing others.[2]

With better healthcare, more of us will be living longer. And as Lam has mentioned, our later years could be the most significant years of our lives. The fact that our energy levels at that chapter of life may not be the same as when we were younger makes it even more important that we have clarity as to what the Lord has called us to do, so that we can invest our energies strategically. Indeed, studies on ageing have shown that "one of the prime predictors of health and well-being in old age is whether a person continues to be purposeful."[3]

It would seem then that clarity about one's life purpose is important at every stage of life.

Followers of Jesus will understand that our life purpose is given to us by God Himself. It is what He calls us to do. It is our vocation.

> Central to the many Christian interpretations of vocation is the idea that there is something—my vocation or calling—God has called me to do with my life, and my life has meaning and purpose at least in part because I am fulfilling my calling.[4]

The subject of calling is a big one and this book is not an attempt to answer every question about vocation. Its goal is a more modest one. This book is an attempt to provide some biblical and practical help for those who want to discover what God may be calling them to do with their lives.

Chapter 1 presents the case for the concept of personal callings. Chapter 2 seeks to explore how one may actually go about discovering one's calling. Chapters 3 to 5 look at three indicators of calling: Ability, Burden, and Critical life incidents. Chapter 6 looks at the various contexts where vocation can be practised. We will see that our vocation is important but that we build our lives not around vocation but around the God who calls us. In "Putting It All Together", you will find the various principles of vocational discernment integrated as a guide for someone to embark on a journey of vocational discovery.

Each chapter is built around three sections. The first section, "Life", gives some incidents from the author's life that led to his reflecting on the subject of that chapter. The second section, "Lessons", gives an overview of key biblical material and insights in the literature on the subject of the chapter. A last section, "Living it out", is a closing exhortation and provides practical handles for how to live out the implications of the chapter.

This book is offered with the hope that it will help more of us to say at the end of our lives:

> I have brought you glory on earth by finishing the work you gave me to do.
> (John 17:4)

1

What Is Calling?

Why am I here? When we can't answer that daunting question, we drift through life, which becomes a succession of loosely linked episodes.[1]

LIFE • LESSONS • LIVING IT OUT

In my final year of dental school, I began to believe that I was called to be a pastor, not a dentist. I have always believed that God calls each of us to different work and I never saw church-related work as more spiritual than other work.

Still, I had to deal with the fact that I was now beginning to feel that I was called to pastoral work. This was a crisis of faith because for the first time in my life I had to pay a price for following Christ.

First, by giving up dentistry, I was giving up a job that promised a generous income, something that was very important for baby-boomer diaspora Chinese like myself. More importantly, my parents would be against such a change. They had sacrificed a lot to put me through dental school.

I didn't want to disappoint them. Therefore, I had to take a long hard look at my Christian faith. It had to be true for me to make this drastic change in my life trajectory. After a few months of intense reflection, I concluded that the Christian faith was indeed true. Jesus was my Lord and

Saviour. Consequently, I had to do whatever He wanted me to.

Next, I had to think through what "calling" meant. After much study of the Bible and extensive reading of key books on the subject, I concluded that God does indeed call us to different life missions. I also came to the conclusion that following one's calling is an expression of stewardship, a principle laid out in 1 Peter.

> Each of you should use whatever gift you have received to serve others, as faithful stewards of God's grace in its various forms. (1 Peter 4:10)

The question, then, was what vocation would allow me to be the best steward of the gifts and abilities God had graced me with? In particular, was I called to the pastorate?

LIFE • **LESSONS** • LIVING IT OUT

The first mission given to humankind was: "Be fruitful and increase in number; fill the earth and subdue it." (Genesis 1:28a) This was a mission that neither Adam nor Eve could have done on their own. Each had a unique contribution to make to conceive the children who would "fill the earth and subdue it." This seems to be the divine pattern. God has a mission, He raises a community to be servants of that mission, and the different members of that community have different roles to play in the pursuit of that mission.

In the New Testament God raises His church to serve His purposes. Paul compares the church to the human body that can only function when the different parts play their respective roles (1 Corinthians 12; Ephesians 4:15–16). We see here the same pattern at play. God has a mission. He raises up a community to serve that mission. Different members of that community have different roles to play to fulfil that mission. All followers of Jesus should be committed to God's mission to be witnesses to Jesus and His work (Luke 24:48) but each of us has different assignments for that mission. We have different callings.

The terms "vocation" and "calling" can be used interchangeably. "Vocation" is just a Latin word for "calling".[2] It begs the question, who is calling whom to do what. And the answer is this: God calls His people to serve Him and assigns each of them their unique personal missions. Calling begins with God. Indeed, our first call is the call to follow Him.

The Primary Call

Our journey to discover our own unique calling must begin with recognising that our first call is to follow Christ.

> Then he called the crowd to him along with his disciples and said: "Whoever wants to be my disciple must deny themselves and take up their cross and follow me." (Mark 8:34)

This primary call encompasses all of life and is true for all followers of Jesus throughout their lives.

> The vocation of every Christian is to live as a follower of Jesus today. In every aspect of life, in small and large acts, with family, neighbor

and enemies, we are to seek to live out the grace and truth of Jesus.[3]

As a follower of Jesus, I am responsible for various roles that I undertake as an expression of love for God and neighbour. They include responsibilities to church (Romans 12:3-8) and family (Ephesians 5:21-6:40), to nation (Jeremiah 29:7), friends (John 15:15-17) and work (Colossians 3:22-4:1). As followers of Jesus, we are to faithfully carry out the tasks that sustain the responsibilities assigned to us. Therefore we do not wait until we are sure of our calling before we live out our lives as followers of Jesus. At all times we are to love God and neighbour in all spheres of life.

Our Special Call

Above and beyond our regular duties, however, we are also called to a mission that is specific to each one of us. Klaus Bockmuehl describes this special call:

> [T]here is, in addition to his or her general (creational) and the special (salvational) assignments, the individual vocation of a Christian to his or her own, separate, personal life work. It comes as a calling to some activity that not every human being and not

every Christian believer is called to, but which is assigned to this particular person.[4]

Gordon T. Smith explains the relationship between our primary calling and our unique personal calling:

> [F]or each individual there is a specific call—a defining purpose or mission, a reason for being. Every individual is called of God to respond through service in the world. Each person has a unique calling in this second sense. We cannot understand this second meaning of the call except in the light of the first. When we fulfil our specific vocation, we are living out the full implications of what it means to follow Jesus.[5]

We see this concept of a personal specific calling in God's call of Jeremiah to his prophetic ministry (Jeremiah 1:4–10). God brought Jeremiah into existence because He had a particular assignment for him. Jeremiah had been set apart "from all other uses to a specific use."[6]

If the call of Jeremiah connects calling with creation, Paul, in the New Testament, connects calling to salvation.

> For it is by grace you have been saved,
> through faith—and this is not from yourselves,
> it is the gift of God—not by works, so that no
> one can boast. For we are God's handiwork,
> created in Christ Jesus to do good works,
> which God prepared in advance for us to do.
> (Ephesians 2:8-10)

The New Testament teaches that we are saved through faith and that we are saved so that we can do work that God prepared in advance for us to do.

> Our vocation is grounded in the self that from
> eternity God has willed that we be. Our calling
> is to become that self and then to serve God
> and our fellow human beings in the particular
> ways that will represent the fulfillment of that
> self.[7]

LIFE • LESSONS • **LIVING IT OUT**

Definitions

I like VantagePoint3's definition of the personal call:

> God invites us to live and serve out of who we are, a vocation or way of life unique to who we have been created and are redeemed to be.[8]

Here are a few other useful definitions of one's personal call:

> Your ... mission here on Earth is one that is uniquely yours, and that is:
>
> a. to exercise the Talent that you particularly came to earth to use—your greatest gift that you most delight to use;
>
> b. in those place(s) or setting(s) that God has caused to appeal to you the most;
>
> c. and for those purposes that God most needs to have done in the world.
>
> Richard N. Bolles[9]

Central to the many Christian interpretations of vocation is the idea that there is something—my vocation or calling—God has called me to do with my life, and my life has meaning and purpose at least in part because I am fulfilling my calling.

William C. Placher[10]

A personal mission statement is a defined, written and constantly revised expression of your unique expression of personal and human vocation that captivates you for service in the world for life. It is more than career and remunerated occupation. It is that service for which we believe we are sent, and sent by God Himself.

R. Paul Stevens[11]

I like the fact that Stevens says that a personal life mission statement, his term for calling, is "a constantly revised expression". It frees us from the need to chase a final and absolute certitude about our calling. It does encourage us to grow in self-knowledge as we move through life, and part of that knowledge is a growing understanding of what might be our unique contribution to God's purposes in the world.

Do note that there is no specific command in the Bible to discover one's calling. However, if the Bible teaches that each of us has unique callings, it makes sense then that we should grow in our understanding of that calling. For many, the first step is to come to the realisation that we each have our unique roles to play in God's purposes.

> The first step for some of us in discovering our unique purpose will be to accept that we have one; that I as an individual have a unique part to play in God's unfolding story.[12]

2

How to Discover My Calling?

A call is an inner desire given by the Holy Spirit through the Word of God and confirmed by the community of Christ.[1]

LIFE • LESSONS • LIVING IT OUT

How does one discover one's specific calling? I graduated from dental school in 1978 and embarked on my dental career. But in the months before my graduation, I was growing in the conviction that my calling lay elsewhere—in serving as a pastor-teacher (Ephesians 4:11)—not because I saw that as more spiritual than dentistry but because that was what I believed God wanted me to do. Still, it represented a major change in my life trajectory. I needed to be sure. I looked to the scriptures for help but found no explicit teaching on how to discover my calling. But I discovered a wealth of biblical wisdom to guide me in my search.

LESSONS

Preparation of the Heart

How does one go about discerning one's calling? We begin by first preparing our hearts. Any journey to discern our calling must begin with a commitment to pursue that calling when it is made clear to us. If our attitude is one of curiosity—we want to know our calling but there is no commitment to actually do it—we shouldn't be surprised that the heavens are silent. That is why God had to prepare Moses so that he would be ready to receive his call at the burning bush.

> Now Moses was tending the flock of Jethro his father-in-law, the priest of Midian, and he led the flock to the far side of the wilderness and came to Horeb, the mountain of God. There the angel of the Lord appeared to him in flames of fire from within a bush. Moses saw that though the bush was on fire it did not burn up. So Moses thought, "I will go over and see this strange sight—why the bush does not burn up."
>
> When the Lord saw that he had gone over to look, God called to him from within the bush,

"Moses! Moses!"

And Moses said, "Here I am."

"Do not come any closer," God said. "Take off your sandals, for the place where you are standing is holy ground." Then he said, "I am the God of your father, the God of Abraham, the God of Isaac and the God of Jacob." At this, Moses hid his face, because he was afraid to look at God. (Exodus 3:1–6)

We must be in a posture of submission before we are ready to receive God's call. Jesus states this principle in John 7:17,

Anyone who chooses to do the will of God will find out whether my teaching comes from God or whether I speak on my own.

The first step in discovering our calling is the choice to do the will of God.

Spiritual Resources for Discernment

There are times when God conveys His calling in dramatic ways, for example the experience of Moses at the burning bush (Exodus 3) or Paul encountering the risen Christ on the Damascus Road (Acts 9:1–19). Clearly these were special calls for special people at special times in salvation history. However, nowhere does the Bible teach that such special callings are the norm. In fact, there is little direct teaching regarding how one can discern one's calling. Instead of a method, God has given us resources to guide us. And there are spiritual disciplines that can help us tap into those resources.

God has given us at least three resources to help His people discern His will. The first resource He has provided us is His Spirit. In John 16:13a, Jesus said: "But when he, the Spirit of truth, comes, he will guide you into all the truth." The first resource for discerning God's will is God Himself. Discerning our calling is not something we do alone. God Himself is with us in the third person of the Trinity, the Holy Spirit.

> In discovering our life calling, we see that God promises to guide us step-by-step over time through the work of the Holy Spirit. (cf. Psalm 23:3, 25:9; Isaiah 48:17; Jeremiah 10:23)[2]

The second resource the Lord has provided to help us discern our calling is the Bible, the Word of God. Commenting on 2 Timothy 3:14–17, Bruce Waltke writes:

> The Scriptures are given to us to teach. That means the Lord gave us the Bible to help us learn how to do things.[3]

The Bible helps us in our call discernment in at least two ways. First, it gives us clear understanding on the whole subject of calling.[4] Next, the Spirit uses the Bible to guide us by bringing our attention to the parts that are relevant to our quest. Here the Spirit and the Word work together, fulfilling Jesus' promise that the Spirit will guide us to the truth.

The third resource the Lord gives us for call discernment is the community of believers. Gordon T. Smith writes:

> [W]e cannot effectively address any of these (vocational) questions on our own. We need the grace of good, clear, honest conversation, without flattery or cliché. We need to be in conversation with women and men, both the community of peers and those older than ourselves....[5]

The wisdom of Proverbs 15:22 holds true for call discernment as well. "Plans fail for lack of counsel, but with many advisers they succeed."

God helps us to discern our calling by providing us with His Spirit, His Word, and His Community.

LIFE • LESSONS • **LIVING IT OUT**

Spiritual Disciplines for Discernment

In his primer on the spiritual life, *Making All Things New*, Henri Nouwen points out that there are two fundamental spiritual disciplines needed for our life in Christ. The first is solitude.

> Without solitude it is virtually impossible to live a spiritual life. Solitude begins with a time and place for God, and him alone. If we really believe not only that God exists but also that he is actively present in our lives—healing, teaching, and guiding—we need to set aside a time and space to give him our undivided attention.[6]

If God has given us His Word and His Spirit to guide us, we need solitude to hear what He is saying to us through His Word and His Spirit. We must set aside space and time to listen to Him. The place of solitude and prayer in decision-making is modelled by Jesus Himself. For example, Jesus sought out His Father in solitude before He decided who would be His initial 12 disciples (Luke 6:12–16). Sometimes, like Elijah in 1 Kings

19, we have to be patient and let the loud noises in our lives die down before we can hear the "gentle whisper" (1 Kings 19:9–13a). If we are serious about discerning what God's calling for us might be, we must commit ourselves to times of solitude when we can hear Him.

The second spiritual discipline that Nouwen says we need is community. He says:

> Community as discipline is the effort to create a free and empty space among people where together we can practice true obedience.[7]

Again, Waltke is helpful. He reminds us of why we need to seek God's guidance in community.

> It is necessary to have a number of counsellors to offset the weaknesses, ignorance, and limitations of each individual. Each resolution succeeds because it emerges out of humility and trust as members submit themselves to be corrected in open, honest counsel.[8]

So, while we must spend time in solitude to allow the Word and the Spirit to speak, we also need to discern God's calling in community. We need peers, spiritual friends who will share with us what we *need* to hear, not what we *want* to hear. And we will need spiritual mentors and directors who will help us hear the Lord more clearly.

Three Clues to Guide Vocational Discernment

We are grateful for God's resources for discernment and the spiritual disciplines that help us to tap on those resources. But are there any clues to guide our discernment? I believe there are three: What is my primary ability, what is my main burden, and what are the critical incidents that have shaped my life?

The first clue is this: What is my primary Ability?

> [W]e can note that some are multitalented, they do two or three things well. Yet, over time it becomes apparent that there is one strength, one capacity that is closer to the root of their being, closer to their heart, and something they must do if they are going to be who they were created to be.[9]

My calling must enable me to be a good steward of my main strength.

The second clue is this: What is my main **B**urden?

> We often ask why the world is the way it is—
> why there is suffering, why there is pain, why
> there is distortion—but some people will feel
> more righteously angry about some issues
> than others, and this may be just their unique
> purpose.[10]

There are many needs in a fallen world. Is there a burden that I am particularly concerned about? My calling must allow me to be a good steward of my primary burden.

The third clue is this: what are the **C**ritical life incidents that have shaped my life? What are the defining moments that have made me who I am? As Dan Allender puts it:

> Listen to your stories. They reveal a pattern
> of roles you've played throughout your life. ...
> [T]he being that a person is at age three still
> has some overlap with the inner world of that
> same person at age ninety-three. A coherent
> sense of self lasts over a lifetime, and what is
> retained over a lifetime speaks to the unique
> role or character you are to play out on God's
> stage. What lasts, yet grows and matures to

an even greater glory, reveals your thematic calling.[11]

My calling must allow me to be a good steward of the experiences that have shaped me.

These then are the A, B, C of our discernment as we reflect on what our unique life mission might be: A—Abilities; B—Burdens; C—Critical life incidents.

Discovering our calling then is a call to pay attention to our lives. In personal reflection and with the help of trusted friends, we look out for what we do well, what we are concerned for, and for guidance from the experiences that have defined us. In this way we "look carefully at hard data that is specific to you."[12] In the following chapters we take a closer look at the three vocational clues.

What Is My Primary Ability?

Giftedness is not about what you can do but what you were born to do, enjoy doing, and do well.[1]

LIFE • LESSONS • LIVING IT OUT

Michael Quah was my Grade 7 form teacher. He was also my arts and crafts teacher. But I was poor in art. My paintings looked like those done by someone in Grade 1 or 2. And in my first attempt at wood carving I stabbed myself with a chisel and lost enough blood to give my parents and my teachers a scare.

Mr. Quah also pushed me to do public speaking. And to write. He told me later that he saw that I had gifts in those areas that were, in his own words, "gushing to burst into life". At 12, I had no idea at all that I had those gifts. I will always be grateful to Mr. Quah for helping me recognise them. My gifts in writing and especially in speaking would be affirmed again and again by many through the years. Because they are gifts from God, there is no place for pride, but our calling should allow us to do what we do best. For me, it meant that I had no career in painting or sculpting. But I write and I speak.

LESSONS

Core Competency

The first clue to what our calling might be is clarity about what we do well. There are many things we need to do, whether we are gifted to do them or not. For example, I am not good at handling finances, but when my wife died I became a single parent and had to oversee the family finances. I learnt to do it as well as I could.

There is also the fact that some of us can do a number of things well. But as Richard N. Bolles suggests, there is a single strength that stands out. He says that our calling must be one that allows us "To exercise the Talent that you particularly came to earth to use—your greatest gift, which you most delight to use."[2]

We have been specifically commanded to be good stewards of our talents (Matthew 25:14–30). Our calling must allow us to be good stewards of our abilities, especially our primary ability—what we do best.

Serve with Your Gifts—A Biblical Principle

Scripture is clear that different people have been given different strengths and we are to serve with the strengths we have been given. Romans 12:4–8 reads:

> For just as each of us has one body with many members, and these members do not all have the same function, so in Christ we, though many, form one body, and each member belongs to all the others. We have different gifts, according to the grace given to each of us. If your gift is prophesying, then prophesy in accordance with your faith; if it is serving, then serve; if it is teaching, then teach; if it is to encourage, then give encouragement; if it is giving, then give generously; if it is to lead, do it diligently; if it is to show mercy, do it cheerfully.

Here is Leon Morris' comment on this passage:

> *Different* brings out the truth that God does not make Christians into a collection of uniform automata. They differ from one another both in their native endowments and also in the gifts that God gives them through the Spirit. The differences are not arbitrary but *according to the grace given us*.[3]

Every member of the church has a unique contribution to make to the life of the church and that unique contribution depends on what gift(s) he or she has been given. As Morris has implied, the fact that it is God who chooses what gift to endow someone with carries with it a sense of responsibility. The gifts and talents that God chooses for us are clues to what He wants us to do.

This principle of people making unique contributions based on their abilities was already seen in the Old Testament. We note for example the construction of the tabernacle in the book of Exodus. Bezalel and Oholiab were selected to work on the ark of the covenant because of their abilities (Exodus 31:1-11; 36:1-4) which the Lord had given them. We see here the principle that we later see in Romans 12. God chooses His servants and gives them their abilities. These abilities then qualify them for the work they are called to do.

Spiritual Gifts and Natural Abilities

It is useful to know that our abilities come in different forms. Spiritual gifts are abilities given to us by the Holy Spirit. "Now to each one the manifestation of the Spirit is given for the common good." (1 Corinthians 12:7) Spiritual gifts are abilities we have by virtue of our salvation. When we repented and responded to the gospel, we became new creations. Indwelt now by the Spirit, we are also empowered by the Spirit to serve and He manifests different gifts in each of us to do that.

But we also have natural talents and abilities that are ours by virtue of our creation. We are all born with different strengths. As Diane J. Chandler reminds us:

> Like spiritual gifts, natural endowments such as talents, abilities and skills are God-given and to be applied in serving others. For example, some may have natural musical, language, financial, athletic or technological abilities that can be offered to serve others and glorify God.[4]

We must not confuse spiritual gifts and natural talents. We have the latter because of creation and the former because we are now God's new creation. But all our abilities are from God, for others, and for His glory. Our primary ability may be a spiritual gift or a natural ability or, as is often the case, some combination of both. When we have clarity as to our primary ability, we will begin to have some clarity regarding our calling.

LIFE • LESSONS • **LIVING IT OUT**

Discovering Your Primary Ability

There is no biblically prescribed formula for discovering one's primary ability. But as we have seen, there are two basic spiritual disciplines that can help most of us discern our primary strengths—solitude and community. In solitude, we give ourselves to personal reflection. In community, we seek communal guidance.

Personal Reflection

If our vocation comes from God it makes sense that we carve out time to attend to His promptings and to hear His voice. In particular, we want to take as objective as possible a look at our lives to ferret out evidence of what we do well. There are two specific exercises we could do to further help us to have greater clarity about our primary strengths. First, we could use assessment tests to help clarify our reflection. There are many talent assessment tests available. Two are worthy of mention. Peter Wagner's *Discover Your Spiritual Gifts* has helped many generations embark on their journey of discovering their spiritual gifts.[5]

Similarly, Tom Rath's *StrengthsFinder 2.0* has also been instrumental in helping many discover their primary strengths.[6] The thing to bear in mind is that we should not treat the results of such self-assessment tests as the voice of God and therefore infallible. They work best as tools to help us reflect on our lives. And they should be done with the help of friends and mentors who can provide honest feedback. Nevertheless, a good self-assessment tool can be very helpful to start you on a journey of discovering your primary gifts.

Another exercise that helps you recognise your strengths is to look back at your life and also stories in your life that indicate a pattern of giftedness.[7] Think of instances in your life when you were doing something and:

- You did it well and enjoyed doing it.
- You lost all sense of time.
- It made a significant impact in the lives of people and/or organisations.
- People said you did well.
- It gave you a deep sense of satisfaction.

Bill Hendricks helps us to identify tell-tale stories in our lives that give us clues to our giftedness.

Maybe you can remember a scene from your childhood, or maybe it's something that happened as recently as last week. When it took place isn't what matters. What matters is that it was a moment in your life that met two criteria: (a) you were actually doing something (as opposed to just passively experiencing something, like watching a TV show or visiting the mountains in Colorado), and (b) you took satisfaction from the activity. You enjoyed doing it. You gained energy from doing it.

The satisfaction is the key. The tell-tale sign that your giftedness is engaged in an activity is that you take joy or satisfaction in doing it.[8]

We will explore the exercise of reflecting on your personal history in more detail in Chapter 5, but we can begin the exercise when we look for patterns of giftedness in our life story.

Communal Guidance

The other discipline that will be key in helping you discern your primary abilities is the discipline of being in community. Gordon T. Smith states it well:

We ask the questions of ourselves, and each of us needs to foster our own, individual capacity to respond to the question of self-knowledge and identity. But it is also important to stress that our self-knowledge and self-awareness happen in community. We come to know ourselves not in isolation from others but as part of the body of Christ.[9]

We discern our vocation—including discerning our primary strengths—in community; in conversations with friends and family who know us well enough to give us honest feedback as we share our tentative conclusions from our personal reflections. What are particularly helpful are mentors who can help guide us as we seek to discern our primary abilities. Diane J. Chandler reminds us that "[m]entors serve as mirrors to reflect one's talents, skills and goals, as well as provide feedback in decision making."[10]

I recall there was a time when I had to choose between a pastoral position and a teaching position. A good friend pointed out that I was better at teaching than in giving pastoral care. It was a key insight that helped me make a wise decision.

It needs to be said that we can't be doing only what we enjoy doing or only what we do well. To love God and to love people in all the spheres of our lives necessitates that we have to do many things and we will seek to do them as best we can. However, it is also true that we are gifted to do certain things well. Hence, discovering those things, especially our primary gift, is an important first step to understanding the purpose of our lives.

What has God called me to do? The first step in answering that question is to come to some clarity about what God has gifted me to do well. We look for our **A**, our primary ability. As Os Guinness reminds us, it is a vital clue to our calling:

> God normally calls us along the line of our giftedness, but the purpose of giftedness is stewardship and service, not selfishness.[11]

GROUP ACTIVITY

Play the recap video by scanning the QR code.

Share your thoughts on the following questions.

1. What is the attitude with which we should view our abilities?

2. Can you recall a time when you did something well, enjoyed doing it, and saw the positive impact that it left on people or organisations?

3. What are the differences and similarities between our spiritual gifts and natural abilities?

What Is My Primary Burden?

First, regarding passion, self knowledge includes the capacity to respond to such questions as, what do I want and what matters to me?[1]

LIFE • LESSONS • LIVING IT OUT

I was in my final year of dental school. I was soon to graduate and commence my career as a dentist. But there was one thing that had bothered me for some time and continued to bug me—the poor quality of Bible teaching in the church. Indeed, I had been concerned for the quality of teaching in the church since my first real encounter with Christ about eight years before that. One fateful evening in my final year of dental school, I voiced to one of my mentors that I was really disturbed by the poor teaching in church. It was a conversation that would lead to the realisation that my persistent burden for good Bible teaching was a major clue to my calling. I did go on to finish dental school. Dental school was tough but I became a competent dentist. However, I was never as burdened for dental health, important as that was, as I was for the health of Bible teaching in church. A number of my dental classmates who were also followers of Jesus were burdened for the practice of good dentistry. That was their calling. Bible teaching was mine.

LESSONS

If the first step in discerning your vocation is to know your primary ability, the second is to discover, in a world with many needs, which of those needs matter most to you.

A World with Many Needs

In John 20:21b, Jesus tells His disciples, "As the Father has sent me, I am sending you." This is a mission that is for all followers of Jesus. As we follow Christ into the world, we discover a fallen world with many needs. Christ has come to make all things new (Revelation 21:5). He has made this possible by His death on the cross, and we now await His return to complete His mission. A key component of the Christian mission is evangelism, to proclaim the good news of Jesus Christ. But as Jonathan Lunde writes:

> Jesus also instructs his disciples to go beyond mere proclamation. Since God's kingdom was arriving in fulfilment of his historical actions of deliverance, Jesus's disciples were to demonstrate its presence in tangible ways that image its presence. Proclamation and

demonstration—these dimensions belong inextricably together.[2]

God's people are to witness to Christ and His mission through both proclamation and demonstration. We are called to proclamation—to share the gospel—and to demonstration—showing God's love and character in all areas of life. In the words of Gordon T. Smith:

> God is calling women and men into every sphere and sector of society. The in-breaking of the reign of Christ happens not so much Sunday morning as it does Monday as the members of the church fan out to fulfill their God-given vocations in the world.[3]

This task of witnessing to Jesus and the kingdom is way beyond any one individual Christian. So, while all of us should be sharing the gospel, vocationally we have different assignments.

Burden as Guide

There are many needs in a broken world and, while all of us should be burdened for all of God's concerns, no single individual can carry the responsibility for the total mission of God. Steven Garber reminds us that "[n]one of us can care for everything everywhere. So we choose to care about something somewhere."[4]

Which is why the Lord has given each of us a primary burden, one need out in the world that specifically speaks to us. Gordon T. Smith summarises this aspect of vocational discernment:

> Where do you see the brokenness of the world; what impresses you to the core of your heart and calls you to be or to do something? When you are able to set aside ego gratification and ask honestly what you long to do to make a difference because you see the need—quite apart from monetary return or honor that might come your way—what comes to mind?[5]

Scripture points us to various individuals with different burdens. In 1 Timothy 3:1, Paul notes that there are those who are burdened for leadership. Paul had a burden for the lost. God sent him to preach the gospel to the Gentiles (Acts 22:21) but he continued to have a deep passion to see his fellow Jews saved (Romans 9:1-3). Moses had a burden to see his people free from slavery. Joseph had a burden to lead from a young age. One vital clue to our vocation, then, is what burden is foremost in our hearts.

I know of a couple that has a burden for creation care. They both had good jobs in the corporate sector but, as time passed, it became very clear that their primary burden was creation care. They are active in their local church and they take seriously their responsibilities as parents. In other words, they are trying to follow Christ in all the dimensions of their lives. But vocationally, they want to see society be better stewards of the environment. And they devote the bulk of their working life to that. All of us are to be concerned for all of God's concerns, but each of us has been entrusted with different burdens.

Burden and Passion

As we have seen, another way of looking at burden is to see what we are passionate about. Often we will experience great joy when we passionately pursue vocations that allow us to address our deepest burdens. Diane J. Chandler writes:

> [O]ur sense of calling is often informed by a burden, passion, compassion, desire or sensitivity to a specific group or cause that propels us to act.[6]

In fact, one's passion or burden may be more important as an indicator of calling than one's strength or talent. Our vocation must give us the opportunity to do what we do best, but where should one apply his or her strength? In the things that mean the most to us. Jerry Sittser writes:

> For whatever reason, some people seem to have an inner compulsion or drive that propels them towards a calling. Something deep within motivates them to start a new business or to compose a symphony or to teach in an inner city school, as if they have to do it, not only because they have a talent for it, which every calling requires, but also because they have the interest, energy, and passion for it. It is simply in them.[7]

Discerning Your Primary Burden

Our primary burden should be self-evident. But most of us would still need help in discovering or clarifying our primary burden. We turn again to personal reflection and communal guidance.

LIFE • LESSONS • **LIVING IT OUT**

Personal Reflection

To find out what is the main burden the Lord has laid on our hearts, we need to listen to our hearts in the presence of God. Here are some questions that can help us reflect:

- What needs in the world really disturb you?
- What needs in the world would you like to focus on?
- What things/issues do you daydream about or wish you had more time to put energy into?
- What do you care deeply about?
- What would you like to invest your life in?
- Which group in the world are you burdened for?

I like Gordon T. Smith's suggestion that we look at what needs in the world make us angry.

> What ... makes a person angry—not in the sense of loss or temper or irritation when she is crossed, but rather the anger she feels when

her heart is aligned with the purposes of God
in the world. What breaks the heart of God—
for this person?[8]

In other words, with all the needs out there in the world, which are the ones that really bug you? I remember that from a young age I was disturbed by the fact that most of the teaching I encountered in the church was poor. Not surprisingly, I ended up as a teacher of the Word. I have already mentioned the couple who are really passionate about creation care. I know of a brother who is passionate about practising cutting-edge dentistry. I know of another couple who live for feeding the homeless. I have a few friends who are burdened to start businesses that provide goods or services at reasonable prices while providing much-needed employment in the areas where their businesses are located.

All of us should be concerned for all of God's concerns. But all of us have been given one concern that we care for more than the other concerns. I like the way Ayo and Ruth Afolabi frame this point:

> In trying to determine the particular jigsaw puzzle piece that I am in God's big picture, I have found one question particularly

helpful: what question is it that I am on earth to answer? Of course, for many of us there will be questions (plural) but the sentiment remains the same.

We often ask why the world is the way it is—why there is suffering, why is there pain, why is there distortion—but some people feel more righteously angry about some issues than others, and this may just be their unique purpose.[9]

We invest time for prayer and reflection to gain clarity about what that primary issue is. And we seek the help of others to reach that clarity.

Communal Guidance

Steven Garber reminds us: "We discover who we are—and what we are meant to do—face to face and side by side with others in work, love and learning."[10]

Face to face: We need mentors who will walk with us to help us clarify our callings, including coming to understand our primary burden. By asking the right questions and sharing wisdom, mentors can help us unmask false burdens and help us clarify our real ones.

Side by side: As we noted earlier, the quest of clarifying our calling is a communal one. Community can help provide a context for peer mentoring but also a relational framework to provide the encouragement we need to live vocationally.

The Christian life is defined by the twin loves for God and for neighbour (Mark 12:28–31). That means followers of Jesus Christ will be concerned by the things He is concerned about. Of all these things we should be concerned for, we look for our primary burden.

Our calling will be defined by our aptitude and our burden. How they converge is shaped by the concrete opportunities that shape our lives. As Chandler reminds us, "... calling develops over time when God-given desire meets aptitude and opportunity."[11]

We needn't be in a hurry. At any given point in time we should seek to live our lives to the fullest for God and for others. But, with time, we should also be clearer about our aptitude and our desire.

GROUP ACTIVITY

Play the recap video by scanning the QR code.

Share your thoughts on the following questions.

1. What needs in the world really disturb you?

2. With your perceived abilities, what role could you play in addressing these needs?

3. How would your contribution make a difference in these particular areas?

5

What Are My Critical Life Incidents?

If God speaks to us at all other than through such official channels as the Bible and the church, then I think He speaks to us largely through what happens to us ....[1]

LIFE • LESSONS • LIVING IT OUT

Our lives are stories. What we become is shaped by the things that happen to us in our stories, that is, the critical incidents that define our lives. I recall that on two different occasions, people who prayed for me told me that they believed that I had been called to a ministry of prophetic teaching. I understood what they meant. My teaching would not just be the passing on of biblical content. My teaching would involve the right content, at the right time, to the right people, for the right purpose. I already had some inkling that that would be my main ministry but these two incidents helped confirm it. What I didn't see coming was the death of one wife, a divorce, and a period of clinical depression. Prophetic teaching needed me to know the Word. It also needed me to know life. In retrospect, I see now how all these critical incidents helped me understand my vocation and helped me carry it out. The third clue to what God may be calling us to do can be gleaned from the critical moments in our lives.

LESSONS

The philosopher-theologian Søren Kierkegaard said:

> Life can only be understood backwards; but it must be lived forwards.[2]

Indeed, life can only be lived forward, but it is in looking back that we find evidence of what the Lord may want us to do with our lives. In examining the details of our lives, we receive greater clarity regarding what we do well and what we are particularly burdened about. As we look backwards, we also look for the critical moments that shaped who we are.

The Crucibles of Life

In their book, *Leading for a Lifetime*,[3] Warren G. Bennis and Robert J. Thomas set out to study the factors that gave rise to the leaders of "today and tomorrow". This was one of their key findings:

> We found that every leader in our study, young or old, had undergone at least one intense transformational experience. That

transformational experience was at the very heart of becoming a leader. The descriptive term we found ourselves using is crucible.[4]

Bennis and Thomas go on to say this about such defining experiences:

> [C]rucibles are places where essential questions are asked: Who am I? Who could I be? Who should I be? How should I relate to the world outside myself? ... Crucibles are, above all, places or experiences from which one extracts meaning, meaning that leads to new definitions of self, and new competencies that better prepare one for the next crucible.[5]

We need to take a good look at our lives to identify our "crucibles" and for clues to our life mission.

Examining Our Story

The hard work of investigating our life story for clues to our calling is based on a number of convictions. First is seeing each of our lives as a story. Indeed, "We tell ourselves stories in order to live."[6] But I believe that the story is not merely a needed metaphor to understand life. I agree with Daniel Taylor when he writes:

Seeing our lives as stories is more than a powerful metaphor. It is how experience presents itself to us. By better understanding story, and our role as characters, we can live more purposefully the kind of life that will give our own story meaning.[7]

Next, we need to believe that God is the Author of our story. He is not only our Creator and Saviour. He authors our story. God is intimately involved in the writing of the story of your life.[8]

Psalm 139:16 tells us:

> Your eyes saw my unformed body;
> all the days ordained for me were written in
> your book before one of them came to be.

Commenting on the verse above, Bruce K. Waltke and James M. Houston wrote, "God foreordains a person's narrative as one swift movement and unity."[9]

However, Waltke and Houston were also quick to warn us that this truth "must be held in tension with the doctrine of human accountability."[10]

Since God is the Author of our life story, our life has meaning and purpose, and we can examine our lives for the purpose He has imbued into our stories. Randy D. Reese and Robert Loane summarise it well:

> [W]e are a unique story. Who we are today or tomorrow is inextricably linked with what has come before: our culture, family, circumstances, choices, location and so forth.[11]

The story of Joseph in Genesis powerfully illustrates how we can see meaning and purpose from our lives. In Genesis 50, Joseph's father passes away. His brothers who had plotted to kill him and who eventually sold him into slavery, are now in his power. The brothers are fearful that Joseph would now take his revenge on them. Instead, this is what Joseph says:

> His brothers then came and threw themselves down before him. "We are your slaves," they said.
>
> But Joseph said to them, "Don't be afraid. Am I in the place of God? You intended to harm me, but God intended it for good to accomplish what is now being done, the saving of many lives. (Genesis 50:18–20)

Joseph reflects on his life, both the good and bad. He realises that God had been the Author of his life, working through all that had happened to him, including his brothers' treachery, to bring him to this point in his life. As a result, he could now carry out his vocation of being a strategic leader, to save Egypt, the surrounding nations, and the people of God, from hunger. He models for us the exercise of reviewing our lives for the critical incidents that define us, with the understanding that God has been sovereignly working through the details of our life.

Marks of a Critical Incident

What are the things that happen to us that qualify as critical life incidents? The personal and subjective nature of defining moments makes it hard to define what would constitute a critical incident. Something that would qualify as a critical incident for one person may not be a defining one for another. Reese and Loane give us a helpful "feel" for what may constitute critical incidents:

> There are critical incidents in a person's life through which God shapes a person. These incidents can be any key relationship or circumstance or event that has significant influence in our shaping. Perhaps it was a gift

given, a promise broken, a skill imparted, an experience on the job, the loving attention of an adult, a trip to another part of the world, and on and on. These events can be both positive and negative. God is sovereign, creative and utterly good. He is able to form and reform our lives even out of the most unlikely and painful circumstances and events we experience.[12]

I have found the work of Angela H. Reed, Richard R. Osmer, and Marcus G. Smucker particularly helpful. They look at lives through *life course theory*, a theory of human growth and development that focuses on the specific events that shape a person's life, and the historical and social patterns in which a person grew up and lived.[13] They ask us to look out for two things—life events and turning points. They define the two types of events in this way.

> A life event is a significant occurrence that marks a person's life. It includes such things as moving, being accepted into college or law school, getting married, starting a successful small business, or receiving an unexpected inheritance from a long-lost aunt. Turning points are major events that lead to a new direction in a person's life story. These include

a conversion experience, the death of a parent or child, losing a job, or getting divorced.[14]

In my life, acceptance into dental school was a life event. The death of my first wife from cancer was a turning point. These and many other events and turning points helped me understand what I was to do with my life. Critical life incidents help in our search for vocational clarity.

LIFE • LESSONS • **LIVING IT OUT**

Discerning Our Critical Moments

There may be times when the Lord dramatically works in our lives to reveal what our defining moments are, but for most of us, most of the time we recognise our critical incidents through the spiritual disciplines of personal reflection and communal guidance.

Personal Reflection

In many ways we are the best people to name what is significant in our lives. It will involve some kind of timeline exercise[15] where we view our life chronologically, from our birth till the present, looking out for our life events and especially for our turning points. In solitude we practise what Richard Peace calls "noticing".

> The spiritual skill one learns in writing a spiritual autobiography is that of noticing. We learn to notice God's presence throughout our lives.[16]

Henson Lim writes about his introduction to the exercise of charting one's timeline:

> My first exposure to charting a personal timeline was when someone blessed me with the book, "Experiencing God" by Henry Blackaby. The terms used were spiritual inventory and spiritual markers.
> It was a very meaningful exercise that helped me make sense of how the Lord had been present in my life, whether I realised it or not. Over the years, this discipline has also helped clarify my kingdom assignments, giving me strength and courage to take the next step.[17]

It is also in the solitude needed for personal reflection that we encounter the Author of our lives—God Himself. We need His help to identify the key stories of our lives and what they mean.

> Solitude is essential for vocational clarity and integrity, because in solitude we are enabled to sustain a connection, a relationship, with the very one who has called us.[18]

There is no way we can rush through such an exercise of "noticing", and we will have to do it a number of times, especially at different chapters of our lives. Each time we do it, it may confirm our trajectory or we may need to do course corrections. It will probably be an exercise that is painful as we revisit painful moments in our lives; moments that have yet to be fully healed. But there will be joyful moments too as we begin to take note of God's blessings and guidance, moments we may not have noticed before or may have forgotten. And because this is an exercise that may surface powerful feelings that may derail us from our main mission, it is advisable that our personal reflections be done with the help of significant others. Thus, discerning our defining moments is an exercise best done with the help of a mentor and/or other spiritual guides.

Communal Guidance

In his book, *Reading Your Life's Story*, Keith R. Anderson reminds us:

> We live in the story that is our house; we live in the stories we tell and believe to be true. Our lives are not merely chronology, timelines or randomly unfolding and unrelated events; they are narrative. We are story. And, in the end, we need others to help us understand and complete the story in which we live.[19]

Most of us will not be able to discover our calling on our own. We need the help of community. In particular, we will need spiritual mentors[20] who can help us detect the fingerprints of the Divine in our lives, folks who will help us sift through the evidence, "listening to the clues and asking questions"[21] to help us see what God has been up to in our lives and what He is telling us through our lives.

This, then, is the third clue in our search for our calling. We need to take a long and careful look at our autobiography to discover the critical incidents that God has allowed in our lives to mature us and to guide us. We look for evidence to help us identify our primary ability and our primary burden. But more than that, we will also be on the lookout for all key incidents that help us understand who we are and what we are called to do.

To do this we need to do the hard work of listening to our own story. Keith Anderson writes:

> Spiritual formation is the process of shaping and retelling our lives within the story of God's action for us. Telling our stories is important, but listening to what we tell in our stories is likewise formational. Listening to

your life is the task of reflecting, pondering, wondering and savoring as a lifelong work. It includes reading the impact of family, community, culture, gender, race and place. It is another way to listen to God's voice.[22]

GROUP ACTIVITY

Play the recap video by scanning the QR code.

Share your thoughts on the following questions.

1. In groups of three or four, spend five minutes each to talk about the critical moments in your timeline. How do you see God maturing you and guiding you through it all?

2. Do your friends see any patterns of giftedness?

3. Can you suggest practical ways in which your family, friends, and mentors can partner you as you clarify your calling?

©

The Practice of Vocation

To believe that a wise and good God is in charge of things implies there is a fit between things that need doing and the person I am meant to be. Finding such a fit, I find my calling.[1]

LIFE • LESSONS • LIVING IT OUT

My father passed away in 2003. The year leading to that was one of the toughest in my life. I was a single father taking care of two boys and living in Petaling Jaya, Malaysia. It was a year when both of them had major government exams and I had to help them prepare for those. Dad was in Penang, 400 kilometers away, fighting congestive heart failure and struggling with diabetic complications. Mum needed my help to discuss dad's case with his doctors and to spend time with dad. So I had to divide my time between Petaling Jaya and Penang, and not really doing justice to either dad and mum, or my boys.

I wasn't focused on my teaching vocation. I was doing all I could to care for family. But life isn't built around vocation, important as that is. Life is built around our relationship with Christ. And He decides how much we are to focus on our vocation at any given chapter in our lives. We are called to our vocations but we are first called to love God and to love neighbour, and to live under the lordship of Christ. In that chapter of my life, to love God and to love neighbour meant I had to lay aside the pursuit of my vocation to care for my family.

LIFE • **LESSONS** • LIVING IT OUT

Choosing to Live Vocationally

If we understand life as a gift and a trust from God, we will choose to live our lives the way He wants us to, not the way we want to. To choose to live our lives vocationally is to say no to living our lives any other way. Therefore we need to intentionally choose how we live our lives.

> We cannot be all things to all people. We need to choose, and our choice will mean saying no to some alternatives and eagerly embracing others.[2]

Indeed, to live vocationally is to die to any attempt to define our lives apart from God and His purposes for us. And as David G. Benner reminds us, to live vocationally is to be truly ourselves, but this fulfilment "lies in the death of our own agendas of fulfilment. It also lies in the crucifixion of all our ego-centred ways apart from complete surrender to God."[3]

The Relativisation of Work

We need to take our vocation seriously. However there is also the danger of building our lives around our vocation and not around the Lord of our vocation. I will always be grateful to Paul Stevens for pointing out this vital truth—that humankind was created on the sixth day of creation, the climax of God's creation of the material world, and they were commissioned to care for creation on God's behalf. But the day after they were created, Adam and Eve could not embark on their important work. Though the word Sabbath is not used, the seventh day of creation was when God ceased from His creative activity and rested. It was not a day for work. It was a day for Adam and Eve to enjoy God's blessings.

> Adam woke up from his unconscious sleep not to start his work of caring for God's world but to experience rest. Adam and Eve's first vocational experience was to waste time for good and for God.[4]

I believe God was making a crucial point when He did this. Humankind was created for important work, but life is more than work. Life is based on our relationship with God. As Paul Heintzman reminds us, citing the work of Alan Richardson, the fact that the seven days of creation climaxes with the Sabbath is a reminder that the chief end of humankind is not to labour but to enjoy God forever.[5] Therefore, while we need to take our vocation seriously, our first call is not to work, and therefore not to vocation. Our first call is to a relationship with the living God. This has to be borne in mind because our pursuit of vocation does not take place in a vacuum. It is impacted by our life circumstances. We will look at some of these circumstances.

Calling and Making a Living

One of the reasons we work is to sustain our lives. Paul says bluntly:

> For even when we were with you, we gave you this rule: "The one who is unwilling to work shall not eat." (2 Thessalonians 3:10)

It would be ideal if the work we do to sustain ourselves also allows us to pursue our vocation. For example, if someone called to be a teacher of the Word works as a pastor of a church and is remunerated for his or her work, he or she makes a living by working at his or her calling. We think of doctors, teachers, artists, etc., whose calling is also the work that sustains them.

But this is not always possible. There were times when Paul sustained himself making tents while pursuing his calling to bring the gospel to the Gentiles. I once knew a brother who was called to write church music. But it was at a time when there was no way he could have made a living from pursuing his craft. He was a trained engineer so he continued to work as an engineer at his day job while he continued to compose church music outside of his office hours. He was a good engineer and he gave his best in his day job. After hours, though, he poured himself into his vocation of composing church music.

LIFE • LESSONS • **LIVING IT OUT**

Calling at Different Chapters of Life

Although each life journey is unique, there are some vocational experiences that tend to appear in different stages of our lives. How we pursue calling will therefore also be impacted by the stage of life we are in. Gordon T. Smith, in his book *Courage & Calling*, looks at what calling may be like at different stages of one's adult life.[6] Here is what I have gleaned from his observations.

Early adulthood (up to 30 years of age)

One begins to take seriously the question of what God wants us to do with our lives. Smith says it is important that one begins to think of what God wants of us and no longer what others—e.g. parents, society, government, church—want.

Mid-adulthood (30–60 years of age)

When one is in his or her mid-thirties, one should have a more mature self-awareness and be much clearer about one's calling, or discover that what we thought was our calling when we were younger was wrong, and we embark on another vocational direction all together.

Senior adulthood (60+ years of age)

This may be the best time to pursue one's vocation. Smith writes:

> This moment in our lives is significant in part because we are able to hear the voice of God without concern for the expectations of peers or organisation, or the pressure of career or employment. We can genuinely step back and see how our loves thus far have been but a prelude.[7]

If we have had to carry many responsibilities in our adult life, retirement from a paid occupation in one's senior years may free one to have more freedom to pursue one's vocation. We note again that we do not equate our vocation with a particular paid job. I have noted for example that women who gave their best to care for their children and/or their husbands, really blossom when their children grow up and move away and/or their spouses pass away, and they are free to come into their own.

Calling and Maturity

Sometimes we are unable to fully carry out our vocation until God has properly shaped our character. Two people in the Old Testament come to mind. Joseph knew early that he was called to leadership. Yet God had to bring him through many years of testing and humbling before He allowed him to become de facto the most powerful person in the most powerful country at that time. We think also of the story of Moses. He was humbled by being a fugitive from Egyptian justice and working as a sheep farmer for 40 years before his calling to free God's people from slavery was activated.

So, while we look for our calling among the A, B, and C of our lives, God is also concerned that we are mature enough to carry out our calling in all its fullness. I knew I was called to a ministry of teaching early in my adult life and tried my best to carry out my calling. But my experiences of widowhood, divorce, and depression were crucial in shaping my character and therefore my suitability to carry out my calling effectively. As Sheridan Voysey writes: "God uses our afflictions to shape who we are and what we do."[8]

Unable to Pursue One's Calling

There will also be circumstances when it is impossible to carry out one's calling. For example, there are those who are incapacitated by debilitating illness. Or there are those who have to care for folks who are seriously ill and that is a responsibility that takes up all their time. Then there are those who live in times and places where normal life is impossible because of wars and natural disasters where the very act of staying alive is a challenge. We think, for example, of the many followers of Jesus who have been imprisoned and tortured for their faith. Their main calling was a call to martyrdom. It is in times like these that we remember that our value and self-worth lie in our relationship with God and not in our work for God.

The following dialogue between DJ and Sheridan Voysey reminds us that work and vocation are not the only things that define us:

> "Not everyone can work," DJ says.
>
> "Exactly. What about the elderly, the unemployed, the chronically ill?"
>
> "What about children?" he adds.

> "Surely their lives have meaning and significance too. Work isn't the only way we express our humanity."[9]

We must always bear in mind then that our primary call is to follow Jesus. Our first loyalty is to Him and not to our vocation. It is God who decides when our time on earth is over and our pursuit of our vocation on earth has come to an end. God also decides when, if, and how much we are to pursue our vocation at any given time in our lives. So, while it is important that we discover our calling and pursue it, we must never forget that we are, first and foremost, followers of Jesus. We must be God-focused, not vocation-focused.

Summary

Our discussion on calling has come full circle. We are first called to respond to Jesus when He says:

> "Whoever wants to be my disciple must deny themselves and take up their cross and follow me." (Matthew 16:24)

In following Him, we also want to imitate Him when He says:

> "My food," said Jesus, "is to do the will of him who sent me and to finish his work." (John 4:34)

We focus then on doing God's will. Often that means practising our vocation. But not always. We can be sure, however, if we live lives of faithfulness, God will use our lives for His purposes.

> Our whole story, even parts that do not yet "make sense", is ordered and intended. Nothing can happen to us that cannot, by God's sovereignty, be turned into good. (Romans 8:28)[10]

Putting It All Together

We long for what we do to grow out of who we are, for our occupation(s) to be rooted in our vocation. That is the hope of everyone's heart.[1]

LIFE • LESSONS • LIVING IT OUT

During the Covid-19 pandemic, large gatherings, including church worship gatherings, were not allowed. Sermons had to be pre-recorded and then broadcasted at the regular worship times. I had to "preach" like this on a number of occasions. Preaching in this way is not ideal at all. I have always understood preaching as a personal encounter between the preacher and a community in real time. Still, I was grateful that I could continue to carry out my vocation. For some time now, I have come to realise that my vocation is "to see lives transformed through the teaching of God's Word with passion, accuracy, and relevance". I am 65 and there is a certain peace in knowing my calling. Of course it's not just about me. Daily we are reminded that we live in a fallen world with many needs. We all need to step up and do our part as agents of Jesus. It makes sense to see how each of us can best contribute to the common good.

LESSONS

The journey to discovering one's vocation can be summarised into a few key components.

One Conviction

Our starting point is the conviction that God has given each of us a specific life mission.

The world is not as it should be. It is a world that is fallen because of sin, populated by a people that are estranged from God because of that sin. But Jesus Christ, God's Messiah, has come, and through His life, death, and resurrection, has begun the job of making all things new. This is the Good News of the Kingdom. A strategic part of this rescue is the raising up of a new humanity who will be both the first fruits and the instruments of God's in-breaking kingdom.

The members of this new humanity have responded to Jesus' call to follow Him. Each member of this new humanity is a unique individual with his or her unique combination of abilities and burdens. This unique mix of abilities and burdens will guide the individual regarding his or her vocation. It is incumbent then for every follower of Jesus to come to some understanding of their unique calling so that they can be faithful stewards of their lives.

> Our vocation is always a response to a Divine call to take our place in the kingdom of God. Our vocation is a call to serve God and our fellow human beings in the distinctive way that fits the shape of our being.[2]

Questions:

- Do you believe you have a unique calling?
- Do you know what it is?

Three Clues

There are three key clues to what one may have been called to do.

First, we need to look at what we are good at doing. Some of us may be good at a few things but we hunt for that one strength that most defines us. We look for our primary ability. Our vocation will allow us to be a good steward of our primary strength.

Next, and perhaps most importantly, we pay attention to what we are most concerned about. We look out at a world that is broken in many ways. All followers of Jesus should be concerned for all the things that God is concerned for. But God has assigned different primary burdens to each of His followers. When we identify that primary burden we will better understand our calling, as our calling will allow us to be a good steward of our primary burden.

Finally, where each of us is really unique is our individual stories. Each person's life will be defined by his or her unique combination of defining moments—life events and turning points that define each life. We believe that God is the Author of our lives and that He takes the details of our lives and shapes them into a coherent narrative. It may take some time for the shape of that narrative to be clearer and so we are looking at a growing awareness of the plot of our lives. But at any point in our lives we can look at what has already transpired to begin to see the trajectory. Our calling should allow us to be good stewards of our very lives and the critical life events that make up each life.

These then are the three main clues to our calling: our primary **a**bility, our primary **b**urden, and the primary **c**ritical life incidents that define us—our **A, B,** and **C**.

Questions:

- At this point in your life, do you have some understanding of your primary ability and burden?
- What critical moments in your life define you?

One Exercise

Where will we find our **A**, **B**, and **C**? In our life story. Therefore one key exercise for anyone who wants to discover their calling is a timeline exercise. Essentially, it is a bird's-eye view of one's life. You draw a line to represent your life from the day you were born to the time you are doing the exercise. Memory is key. Go through your life story and take note of important life events and turning points in your life. Reflect on those moments. What do they tell you about your strengths? Your primary burden? Look at the critical moments that have defined you. How do they help you understand what you should be doing with your life? Can they help you extrapolate what happens next in your life?

Perhaps the most important of the three clues is **B**—burden. What burden has the Lord laid on your heart? Once that is identified, you will have a clearer picture of where you should apply your primary strength. The critical incidents are guides to the context in which you carry out your primary life mission.

You should do this exercise at various points in your life. With the passing of time, the pattern of your life will get clearer. We are on a journey of greater self-knowledge. But we live in the present. We are stewards of what we know at any given point in time.

> **Questions:**
>
> - If you haven't done a timeline exercise recently, why don't you take this opportunity to do one?
> - What did you learn about yourself?
> - What clues did you glean about your calling?

Three Spiritual Resources

We do not live the Christian life with our own resources. Whatever the Lord calls us to do, He gives us the resources to do it. This includes the quest to discover our calling.

The first resource He gives us is His Spirit. In other words, He gives us Himself. Immanuel, God with us, is with us. As we embark on this journey of self-discovery God Himself journeys with us. He is intimately concerned for our search for vocation. He wants to guide us.

The second resource is His Word. He reveals His heart and mind through the Bible. The Bible helps us in our search in at least two ways. Objectively, the Bible lays out a theology of vocation. Subjectively, certain passages may speak to us more personally. Often the Spirit guides us through the Word.

The third resource is God's people. The Christian life is a communal life. God's Spirit speaks through His Word. He also speaks through His people.

We need these three divine resources not just for vocational discernment. Familiarity and appropriation of these resources should be part and parcel of a life of discipleship. In many ways, clarity of vocation is an expression of our life in Christ.

> **Questions:**
>
> - Are you familiar with the three main resources for discipleship?
>
> - In what concrete ways do you appropriate them in your daily life?

Two Spiritual Disciplines

To avail ourselves of God's resources, we need to be committed to two key spiritual disciplines.

The first is solitude. We need to be quiet before the Lord. We need silence as we look over our lives. We need silence for personal reflection. We need silence to hear what the Spirit is saying to us through His Word. We need silence to discern if what the community is saying to us is from the Lord. As Henri Nouwen reminds us:

> *Lectio divina*, silence, discernment, and spiritual direction are central elements in spiritual formation. Whichever particular "school of prayer" we follow, they all stress that the Word of God needs to be received in solitude and silence ...[3]

The other spiritual discipline we need in our journey to knowing our vocation is *the need to consult the community of believers*. We need the loving, wise input of our brothers and sisters.

> Without community we become individualistic and egocentric. Therefore, spiritual formation always includes formation to life in community.[4]

Guidance can come from those who are further down the road of discipleship—spiritual mentors, spiritual directors, disciplers, etc. But there is also much to be gained from the wisdom of peers, spiritual friends who are walking beside us, folks who love God and who love us and who will tell us the truth.

Gordon T. Smith points us to the same two spiritual disciplines:

> We need two very particular anchors if we are going to grow in self-knowledge and have the courage to see and the humility to accept who we are .... There are no exceptions. The ordered life is structured around and is anchored in two realities: community and solitude.[5]

Questions:

- To what degree are you practising the two main spiritual disciplines of solitude and community?
- Which one is harder for you?
- How can you apply the disciplines in vocational discernment?

LIFE • LESSONS • **LIVING IT OUT**

The starting point of any search for vocation is the desire to be faithful stewards of our lives. Life, and our new life in Christ, are precious gifts from the Lord. We know we are saved by faith, but we do want our lives to count for the Lord who saved us. He has given us all the necessary components to discover our calling. It's up to us to embark on the exciting journey of knowing the purpose of our lives.

David G. Benner ends his book, *The Gift of Being Yourself*, with a useful exercise for vocational discernment. It can be a guide for our own exercise of vocational discernment:

> Prayerfully write out a mission statement for your life. Think back over your life to this point, reviewing the givens of your being and seeking to discern calling within them. Add to this any direct leadings of God you believe yourself to have received. Begin your written statement with the words "Called to …" and allow it to reflect what you feel to be the reason you were created and the unique face

of Christ you have been called to be. Discuss this with someone who knows you well and whom you trust, seeking their perspective but not adopting it as your own unless it is confirmed by prayer and careful reflection.[6]

Conclusion

In his book, *The Fabric of Faithfulness*, Steven Garber poses this question:

> How does someone decide which cares and commitments will give shape and substance to life, for life?[1]

This book is one attempt to answer that question. The question and the answer are needed more than ever. We must come to terms with two extremes where vocation is concerned. On the one hand, we must avoid making vocation the centre of our lives. Our vocation is not some holy grail to be discovered before we get on with life. Vocation is only one dimension of our lives in Christ. We centre our lives on Christ. At any point in time, He decides how we should live and what we should do. Jesus decides to what degree we carry out our calling or if we carry out our calling at all.

However we also want to be good stewards of our uniqueness. Each of us is a unique combination of strengths and passions. Each of us is a story God is writing. We want to take seriously the fact that God created us and that He saved us. We believe He had some purpose in mind when He gave us the gift of existence. Therefore we believe we should live lives vocationally. We want to go through life with our eyes open to what He may have called us to do. We want to live our lives in a way that, God willing, we apply who we are to the common good. Indeed, we believe it is more important than ever that people live vocationally.

Vocation Serves as a Compass in a World Where Employment Is Now in a Constant State of Flux

In their book, *Taking Your Soul to Work*, R. Paul Stevens and Alvin Ung write:

> One thing is certain: we will be in vocational transitions for our whole life. This sense of transition is particularly acute for people in their twenties and thirties, who will likely work at least eight different jobs until retirement.[2]

Stevens and Ung wrote their book in 2010. I suspect the pace of vocational transitions has accelerated since. In contrast, I think of my father who did one job all his working life. Knowing our calling means that even if we have to change jobs, we will still know who we are and what we are called to do. And even when we retire from paid employment, we can still do what we are called to do on a voluntary basis.

Living Life Vocationally Is Critical for Human Thriving

As Emily Esfahani Smith writes in her book, *The Power of Meaning*, knowing one's life purpose is one of the key factors in living a life of meaning. Interestingly she also notes that although a person is healthier when he or she lives with a sense of purpose, that purpose often involves being concerned for others rather than oneself:

> Though living with purpose may make us happier and more determined, a purpose-driven person is ultimately concerned not with those personal benefits but with making the world a better place.[3]

Smith writes from the perspective of sociology and psychology, but, as is often the case, empirical research affirms what we know from the Word. As Jesus said, eternal life is about loving God and loving neighbour.

Living Vocationally Allows Us to Make Our Maximum Impact for God's Purposes

Daily we receive fresh evidence that we live in a fallen and broken world. When this book was written, the world was witnessing horrendous bushfires in Australia, a devastating global pandemic, and aggressive polarisation on the issue of racism. These remind us that creation and society are broken. Unless we choose to close our eyes and our hearts, we will be asking, "What, O Lord, will be my response to the brokenness in our world?"

> I'm neither romantic nor naïve about the barriers that we face, but I'd have to become totally cynical to quit—or else I'd have to become someone else. I just don't know how you can not notice some of the injustices—the wrongs that are in front of you.[4]

Followers of Christ know that our ultimate hope is in Christ's return, and the ultimate solution to the problems of humankind is the gospel of Jesus Christ. But followers of Jesus also pray, "your will be done on earth as it is in heaven." (Matthew 6:10) That surely entails not just preaching the gospel but being involved in the world, doing what we can to make the world a better place while we await His return.

In her book, *The Top Five Regrets of the Dying*, Bronnie Ware notes that one of the top five regrets is this:

> I wish I had the courage to live a life true to myself, not the life expected of me.[5]

Followers of Jesus should be sympathetic to this sentiment. I will add, however, that a life true to one's self is the life that God has called one to. As James Martin writes:

> The most important spiritual insight I've learned since entering the Jesuits is that God calls each of us to be who we are.[6]

In choosing to live vocationally, we seek to be more of who we are—for God and for others.

ENDNOTES

Introduction

1. William Damon, *The Path to Purpose* (New York, NY: Free Press, 2008), 31.
2. Kee-Hing, Lam, *Discover Your Life Purpose* (Malaysia: Pristine World, 2015), 12–13.
3. Damon, *The Path to Purpose*, 26.
4. William C. Placher, *Callings* (Grand Rapids, MI: Eerdmans, 2005), 2.

Chapter 1: What Is Calling?

1. Chris Lowney, *Heroic Living* (Chicago, IL: Loyola Press, 2009), 53.
2. William C. Placher, *Callings* (Grand Rapids, MI: Eerdmans, 2005), 1.
3. Mark Labberton, *Called* (Downers Grove, IL: InterVarsity Press, 2014), 45.
4. Klaus Bockmuehl, "Recovering Vocation Today", in *With Heart, Mind & Strength: The Best of Crux*, 1979–1989 (Langley, B.C.: Credo, 1990), 86.
5. Gordon T. Smith, *Courage & Calling*, Revised & Expanded (Downers Grove, IL: InterVarsity Press, 2011), 10.
6. J. A. Thompson, *The Book of Jeremiah* (Grand Rapids, MI: Eerdmans, 1980), 145.
7. David G. Benner, *The Gift of Being Yourself* (Downers Grove, IL: InterVarsity Press, 2004), 105.
8. VantagePoint3 Team, *The Journey Stage 1: Biblical Foundations* (Sioux Falls, SD: VantagePoint3, 2013), 53. Here, VantagePoint3 is expanding on the work of

Gordon T. Smith's *Courage & Calling*.
9. Richard N. Bolles, *What Colour Is Your Parachute 2018* (Emeryville, CA: Ten Speed Press, 2018), 291.
10. William C. Placher, *Callings*, 2.
11. R. Paul Stevens, *Vocation, Work and Ministry Resource Binder* (Vancouver, B.C.: Regent College, 1996), 57.
12. Ayo & Ruth Afolabi, *MORE>Direction: Navigating the Unique Calling God Has for Your Life* (London, U.K.: Inter-Varsity Press, 2018), 49, 52.

Chapter 2: How to Discover My Calling?

1. Bruce Waltke, *Finding the Will of God* (Gresham, OR: Vision House, 1995), 128.
2. Diane J. Chandler, *Christian Spiritual Formation* (Downers Grove, IL: InterVarsity Press, 2014), 164.
3. Bruce Waltke, *Finding the Will of God*, 76.
4. See Chapter one of this book for an attempt to give an overview of a biblical perspective on vocation.
5. Gordon T. Smith, *Consider Your Calling* (Downers Grove, IL: InterVarsity Press, 2016), 115.
6. Henri J. Nouwen, *Making All Things New* (San Francisco, CA: Harper & Row, 1981), 69.
7. Ibid., 80.
8. Bruce K. Waltke, *The Book of Proverbs Chapters 1–15* (Grand Rapids, MI: Eerdmans, 2004), 633.
9. Gordon T. Smith, *Courage & Calling*, Revised & Expanded (Downers Grove, IL: InterVarsity Press, 2011), 56.
10. Ayo & Ruth Afolabi, *MORE>Direction: Navigating the Unique Calling God Has for Your Life* (London, U.K.: Inter-Varsity Press, 2018), 55.
11. Dan B. Allender, *To Be Told* (Colorado Springs, CO: Waterbrook Press, 2005), 95–96.
12. Alistair Mackenzie, Wayne Kirkland & Annette

Dunham, *Soul Purpose* (Christchurch, NZ: NavPress NZ, 2004), 42.

Chapter 3: What Is My Primary Ability?

1. Bill Hendricks, *The Person Called You* (Chicago, IL: Moody Press, 2014), 33.
2. Richard N. Bolles, *What Colour Is Your Parachute 2018* (Emeryville, CA: Ten Speed Press, 2018), 280.
3. Leon Morris, *The Epistle to the Romans* (Cambridge, U.K.: Apollos, 1988), 440.
4. Diane J. Chandler, *Christian Spiritual Formation* (Downers Grove, IL: InterVarsity Press, 2014), 172.
5. Peter Wagner, *Discover Your Spiritual Gifts*, Updated and Expanded (Ventura, CA: Regal Books, 2012).
6. Tom Rath, *StrengthsFinder 2.0* (New York, NY: Gallup Press, 2007).
7. Two books among many that provide guidance for this exercise are: Bill Hendricks, *The Person Called You* (Chicago, IL: Moody Publishers, 2014) and John B. Samuel & Skip Moen, *Living In Your Zone* (Montverde, FL: Talent Research Foundation, 2011). I am particularly grateful to John B. Samuel who guided me through a significant review of my strengths.
8. Bill Hendricks, *The Person Called You*, 95.
9. Gordon T. Smith, *Courage & Calling*, Revised & Expanded (Downers Grove, IL: InterVarsity Press, 2011), 68.
10. Diane J. Chandler, *Christian Spiritual Formation*, 173.
11. Os Guinness, *The Call* (Nashville, TN: WORD Publishing, 1998), 46.

Chapter 4: What Is My Primary Burden?

1. Gordon T. Smith, *Called To Be Saints* (Downers Grove, IL: InterVarsity Press, 2014), 100.

2. Jonathan Lunde, *Following Jesus, the Servant King* (Grand Rapids, MI: Zondervan, 2010).
3. Gordon T. Smith, *Called To Be Saints*, 207.
4. Steven Garber, *The Seamless Life* (Downers Grove, IL: InterVarsity Press, 2020), 13.
5. Gordon T. Smith, *Courage & Calling*, Revised & Expanded (Downers Grove, IL: InterVarsity Press, 2011), 65.
6. Diane J. Chandler, *Christian Spiritual Formation* (Downers Grove, IL: InterVarsity Press, 2014), 167.
7. Jerry Sittser, *The Will of God as a Way of Life* (Grand Rapids, MI: Zondervan, 2004), 175.
8. Gordon T. Smith, *Called To Be Saints*, 101.
9. Ayo & Ruth Afolabi, *MORE>Direction: Navigating the Unique Calling God Has for Your Life* (London, UK: Inter-Varsity Press, 2018), 54–55.
10. Steven Garber, *The Fabric of Faithfulness*, Expanded Edition (Downers Grove, IL: InterVarsity Press, 2007), 161.
11. Diane J. Chandler, *Christian Spiritual Formation* (Downers Grove, IL: InterVarsity Press, 2014), 164.

Chapter 5: What Are My Critical Life Incidents?

1. Frederick Buechner, *Now and Then* (New York, NY: HarperCollins, 1991), 3.
2. Søren Kierkegaard, Soren Kierkegaard Quotes, BrainyQuote.com, BrainyMedia Inc, 2019. [Accessed on 4 December 2019] https://www.brainyquote.com/quotes/soren_kierkegaard_105030
3. Warren G. Bennis & Robert J. Thomas, *Leading for a Lifetime: How Defining Moments Shape Leaders of Today and Tomorrow* (Boston, MA: Harvard Business School Press, 2007).
4. Ibid., 14.
5. Ibid., 99.

6. Joan Didion, "The White Album," in *We Tell Ourselves Stories in Order to Live*, Collected Nonfiction (New York, NY: Alfred A. Knopf, 2006), 185.

7. Daniel Taylor, *Tell Me A Story* (St. Paul, MN: Bog Walk Press, 2001), 4.

8. Keith R. Anderson, *A Spirituality of Listening* (Downers Grove, IL: InterVarsity Press, 2016), 88.

9. Bruce K. Waltke and James M. Houston, *The Psalms as Christian Worship* (Grand Rapids, MI: Eerdmans. 2010), 562.

10. Ibid.

11. Randy D. Reese & Robert Loane, *Deep Mentoring* (Downers Grove, IL: InterVarsity Press, 2012), 52.

12. Ibid., 63.

13. Angela H. Reed, Richard R. Osmer & Marcus G. Smucker, *Spiritual Companioning* (Grand Rapids, MI: Baker Academic, 2015), 128. They contrast life course theory with life cycle theory, which focuses on predictable crises that people face at the same points in life. Life course theory focuses on the unique events that shape an individual's life.

14. Ibid., 131.

15. See Richard Peace, *Spiritual Autobiography* (Colorado Springs, CO: NavPress, 1998), 65–78 for help in preparing an autobiographical timeline.

16. Ibid., 89.

17. Henson Lim, *Alignment Check* (Singapore: Archippus Awakening, 2018), 272–73. Lim's ministry, Archippus Awakening, has helped many discover their calling, or what he calls kingdom assignments.

18. Gordon T. Smith, *Courage & Calling*, Revised & Expanded (Downers Grove, IL: InterVarsity Press, 2011), 261.

19. Keith R. Anderson, *Reading Your Life's Story* (Downers Grove, IL: InterVarsity Press, 2016), 78.

20. Keith R. Anderson & Randy D. Reese, *Spiritual Mentoring* (Downers Grove, IL: InterVarsity Press, 1999), 36. I like Anderson & Reeses' summary of the dynamic of mentoring: a process of "spiritual formation by which one person becomes a spiritual guide for one or several others". We need such guides to help us see what God is doing in our lives.
21. Randy D. Reese & Robert Loane, *Deep Mentoring*, 46.
22. Keith R. Anderson, *A Spirituality of Listening*, 82.

Chapter 6: The Practice of Vocation

1. William C. Placher, *Callings* (Grand Rapids, MI: Eerdmans, 2005), 3.
2. Gordon T. Smith, *Courage & Calling*, Revised & Expanded (Downers Grove, IL: InterVarsity Press, 2011), 86.
3. David G. Benner, *The Gift Of Being Yourself* (Downers Grove, IL: InterVarsity Press, 2004), 105.
4. R. Paul Stevens, "Sabbath," in *The Complete Book of Everyday Christianity*, edited by Robert Banks & R. Paul Stevens (Singapore: Graceworks Private Limited 2011), 872–73. We are not here entering into the debate as to whether the passage refers to six literal days or six periods of time. We are just taking the sequence as it is.
5. Paul Heintzman, *Leisure and Spirituality* (Grand Rapids, MI: Baker Academic, 2015), 88.
6. Gordon T. Smith, *Courage & Calling*, Revised & Expanded, 78–108.
7. Ibid., 104.
8. Sheridan Voysey, *The Making of Us* (Nashville, TN: Thomas Nelson, 2019), 165.
9. Ibid., 91.
10. R. Paul Stevens, "Vocational Guidance," in *The Complete Book of Everyday Christianity*, edited by Robert Banks &

R. Paul Stevens (Singapore: Graceworks, 2011), 1097.

Putting It All Together

1. Steven Garber, *The Seamless Life* (Downers Grove, IL: InterVarsity Press, 2020), 44.
2. David G. Benner, *The Gift Of Being Yourself* (Downers Grove, IL: InterVarsity Press, 2004), 97.
3. Henri Nouwen, *Spiritual Formation* (New York, NY: HarperCollins, 2010), xxvi.
4. Gordon T. Smith, *Courage & Calling*, Revised & Expanded (Downers Grove, IL: InterVarsity Press, 2011), 256.
5. Ibid., xxvi.
6. David G. Benner, *The Gift Of Being Yourself*, 107. I have found Kevin & Kay Marie Brennfleck's *Live Your Calling* (San Francisco, CA: Jossey-Bass, 2005) a helpful resource to guide one to find and fulfil one's calling.

Conclusion

1. Steven Garber, *The Fabric of Faithfulness*, Expanded Edition (Downers Grove, IL: InterVarsity Press, 2007), 39.
2. R. Paul Stevens & Alvin Ung, *Taking Your Soul To Work* (Grand Rapids, MI: Eerdmans, 2010), 161.
3. Emily Esfahani Smith, *The Power of Meaning* (New York, NY: Crown Publishing, 2017), 90.
4. Laurent A. Parks Daloz, Cheryl H. Keen, James P. Keen & Sharon Daloz Parks, *Common Fire* (Boston, MA: Beacon Press, 1996), 199.
5. Bronnie Ware, *The Top Five Regrets of the Dying* (Carlsbad, CA: Hay House, 2011), 37.
6. James Martin, SJ, *Becoming Who You Are* (Boston, MA: HiddenSpring, 2006), 71.

ABOUT THE AUTHOR

Since 1985, Soo-Inn has been journeying with people through his ministry of preaching/teaching, writing, and mentoring. He is a director of *Graceworks*, a training and publishing consultancy committed to promoting spiritual friendship in church and society. He runs this ministry in partnership with his wife, Bernice. They have four sons.

Originally trained as a dentist at the University of Singapore, he answered God's call to go into full-time church-related ministry in 1981 and obtained his Master of Theology from Regent College, Vancouver, Canada, in 1984. In 2006, he obtained his Doctor of Ministry from Fuller Theological Seminary, California.

He has worked as a dentist, pastored two churches, and served in a number of parachurch organisations. He also serves as an adjunct lecturer in various seminaries in Singapore and Malaysia and has authored several books.

His primary passions include connecting the Word of God to the struggles of daily life, and the promotion of the discipline of spiritual friendship. He has supported Arsenal Football Club since 1971 and his favourite movie is Star Wars 4.

GRACEW◉RKS

Graceworks is a publishing and training consultancy based in Singapore, dedicated to promoting spiritual friendship in church and society, and seeing lives transformed through books that present truth for life.

Our publications can be found on our online store, www.graceworks.com.sg/store.

Get in touch with us at enquiries@graceworks.com.sg, or follow us on Facebook (@GraceworksSG) and Instagram (graceworkssg).

www.ingramcontent.com/pod-product-compliance
Lightning Source LLC
LaVergne TN
LVHW041609070526
838199LV00052B/3060